ANIMAL RHYME TIME!

RHYME TIME WITH BEES!

BY JONAS EDWARDS

Gareth Stevens
PUBLISHING

Please visit our website, www.garethstevens.com. For a free color catalog of all our high-quality books, call toll free 1-800-542-2595 or fax 1-877-542-2596.

Library of Congress Cataloging-in-Publication Data

Names: Edwards, Jonas, author.
Title: Rhyme time with bees! / Jonas Edwards.
Description: New York : Gareth Stevens Publishing, [2021] | Series: Animal rhyme time! | Includes index.
Identifiers: LCCN 2019055664 | ISBN 9781538256084 (library binding) | ISBN 9781538256060 (paperback) | ISBN 9781538256077 (6 Pack) | ISBN 9781538256091 (ebook)
Subjects: LCSH: Bees–Juvenile literature. | Rhyme–Juvenile literature.
Classification: LCC QL565.2 .E39 2021 | DDC 595.79/9–dc23
LC record available at https://lccn.loc.gov/2019055664

First Edition

Published in 2021 by
Gareth Stevens Publishing
111 East 14th Street, Suite 349
New York, NY 10003

Copyright © 2021 Gareth Stevens Publishing

Editor: Kate Mikoley

Photo credits: Cover, p. 1 irin-k/Shutterstock.com; cover, pp. 3–24 (music notes) StockSmartStart/Shutterstock.com p. 5 Mr. Meijer/Shutterstock.com; p. 7 Roomanald/Shutterstock.com; p. 9 Jannarong/Shutterstock.com; p. 11 Hugh K Telleria/Shutterstock.com; p. 13 Zety Akhzar/Shutterstock.com; p. 15 thatmacroguy/Shutterstock.com; p. 17 LilKar/Shutterstock.com; p. 19 bluedog studio/Shutterstock.com; p. 21 0 Lorenzo Bernini 0/Shutterstock.com.

All rights reserved. No part of this book may be reproduced in any form without permission in writing from the publisher, except by a reviewer.

Printed in the United States of America

Some of the images in this book illustrate individuals who are models. The depictions do not imply actual situations or events.

CPSIA compliance information: Batch #CS20GS: For further information contact Gareth Stevens, New York, New York at 1-800-542-2595.

CONTENTS

Let's Learn About Bees!. 4

The Bumblebee 6

Bees Help 8

Pollinators 10

All Kinds of Bees 12

The Leaf-Cutter 14

The Honeybee 16

Bye from the Bees! 20

Glossary. 22

For More Information 23

Index 24

Boldface words appear in the glossary.

Let's Learn About Bees!

Hello, I'm a bee!

Please don't be afraid of me.

I may sting if you get too close.

But helping plants is what I love most.

Come and learn about my friends and me.

There are many kinds of bees to see!

The Bumblebee

As for me, I'm a bumblebee.

I live in a group called a colony.

Females are workers.

Males are called drones.

We have a queen, but there's no **throne**.

We are black, yellow, and fuzzy.

Our wings make a sound—it's kind of buzzy!

Bees Help

Bee stings can hurt, yes that's for sure.

But from far away, you might like us a little more.

You see, we help some plants grow, or thrive.

Just don't get too close to our nest, called a hive.

Pollinators

Plants use flowers to make their seeds.

And flowers are tasty—lucky for me!

I love to eat their pollen and nectar.

You could even call me a pollen **collector**!

Some gets caught on me as I go.

Pollination may happen and help a plant grow.

All Kinds of Bees

When it comes to bees,
there are thousands of kinds.
Here are some other bees
you may find.
There are mason bees and
cuckoo bees.
Carpenter bees chew on dead trees!
These bees aren't where the story ends.
Let's go meet some more bee friends.

CARPENTER BEE

13

The Leaf-Cutter

This bee is known as a leaf-cutter.

With her **jaws**, she cuts leaves like butter.

She sure thinks pollen is yummy.

Sometimes a little gets stuck on her tummy.

When she flies away, it may fall on a flower.

A new flower is born.

That's **reproduction** power!

The Honeybee

If you look over here you'll see,

a group of worker honeybees.

They live together in a hive or nest.

They make honey the very best.

Their waggle dance is a little **groove**.

It tells the others where they

should move.

The honeybee has a part called a crop. Nectar's stored here so they don't waste a drop.

At the nest, they throw up the matter. Into another bee's mouth goes the splatter!

It happens again. The nectar is runny. It goes into a **honeycomb** and will become honey!

Bye from the Bees!

Thanks for buzzing along with us!

We hope you can see you don't need to fuss.

We're no cause for **alarm**.

We don't mean any harm.

If you see us, give us space.

We help make the world a better place!

GLOSSARY

alarm: a feeling of fear caused by a sense of danger

collector: someone who collects, or brings things together

groove: an enjoyable pattern of movement or sound, such as a dance

honeycomb: a group of wax cells filled with honey and built by honeybees in their hive

jaws: the walls of the mouth

pollination: the transfer of plant pollen that results in fruits and vegetables

reproduction: the act of a living thing creating another thing just like itself

throne: the seat of a ruler, such as a king or queen

FOR MORE INFORMATION

BOOKS

Moses, Brian. *Animal Poems*. New York, NY: Windmill Books, 2018.

Raatma, Lucia. *A Colony of Bees*. North Mankato, MN: Pebble, 2020.

Randolph, Joanne. *Poems About Animals*. New York, NY: Windmill Books, 2019.

WEBSITES

Bee Colonies
www.dkfindout.com/us/animals-and-nature/insects/bee-colonies/
Learn more about the groups bees live in here.

Honeybee
kids.nationalgeographic.com/animals/invertebrates/insects/honeybee/
Read more about honeybees on this website.

Why Do Bees Buzz?
www.wonderopolis.org/wonder/why-do-bees-buzz
Find out why bees make their buzzing sound on this page.

Publisher's note to educators and parents: Our editors have carefully reviewed these websites to ensure that they are suitable for students. Many websites change frequently, however, and we cannot guarantee that a site's future contents will continue to meet our high standards of quality and educational value. Be advised that students should be closely supervised whenever they access the internet.

INDEX

bumblebee 6
carpenter bee 12, 13
colony 6
crop 18
cuckoo bee 12
drone 6
hive 8, 9, 16
honey 16, 18, 19
honeybee 16, 18
honeycomb 18, 19
leaf-cutter bee 14
mason bee 12

nectar 10, 18
nest 8, 16, 18
pollen 10, 14
pollination 10
queen 6
reproduction 14
sting 4, 8
worker 6, 16